EXtreme
Animals

# The Strongest Animals

by Catherine Ipcizade

**Consulting Editor:** Gail Saunders-Smith, PhD

**Consultant:** Tanya Dewey, PhD
University of Michigan Museum of Zoology

CAPSTONE PRESS
a capstone imprint

Pebble Plus is published by Capstone Press,
151 Good Counsel Drive, P.O. Box 669, Mankato, Minnesota 56002.
www.capstonepub.com

Books published by Capstone Press are manufactured with paper
containing at least 10 percent post-consumer waste.

*Library of Congress Cataloging-in-Publication Data*
Ipcizade, Catherine.
  The strongest animals / by Catherine Ipcizade.
    p. cm. — (Pebble plus. Extreme animals)
  Includes bibliographical references and index.
  Summary: "Simple text and photographs present the world's strongest animals"—Provided by publisher.
  ISBN 978-1-4296-5309-1 (library binding)
  ISBN 978-1-4296-6212-3 (paperback)
  1. Muscle strength—Juvenile literature. 2. Animals—Juvenile literature. I. Title. II. Series.
QL831.I63 2011
590—dc22                                                                         2010028760

**Editorial Credits**
Katy Kudela, editor; Heidi Thompson, designer; Marcie Spence, media researcher; Laura Manthe, production specialist

**Photo Credits**
Alamy: Arco Images GmbH, cover, infocusphotos.com, 7; Ardea: Chris Harvey, 17, Francois Gohier, 13, Thomas
Marent, 9; iStockphoto: aldra, 1; Minden Pictures: Mike Parry, 5, Thomas Marent, 19; Photolibrary Group/Peter
Arnold, Inc.: John Downer, 15; Seapics: Bob Cranston, 11; Shutterstock: Christos Georghiou, Zheltyshev, 21

## Note to Parents and Teachers

The Extreme Animals series supports national science standards related to life science.
This book describes and illustrates strong animals. The images support early readers in
understanding the text. The repetition of words and phrases helps early readers learn new
words. This book also introduces early readers to subject-specific vocabulary words, which are
defined in the Glossary section. Early readers may need assistance to read some words and to
use the Table of Contents, Glossary, Read More, Internet Sites, and Index sections of the book.

Printed in the United States of America in North Mankato, Minnesota.
092010     005933CGS11

# Table of Contents

# Strong

They squeeze! They chomp!
They crush! These animals aren't
just strong. Their strength
is EXTREME.

A blue whale eats tons of krill.
Swallowing is easy for this giant
whale. Its tongue is strong
enough to hold 50 people!

Mighty!

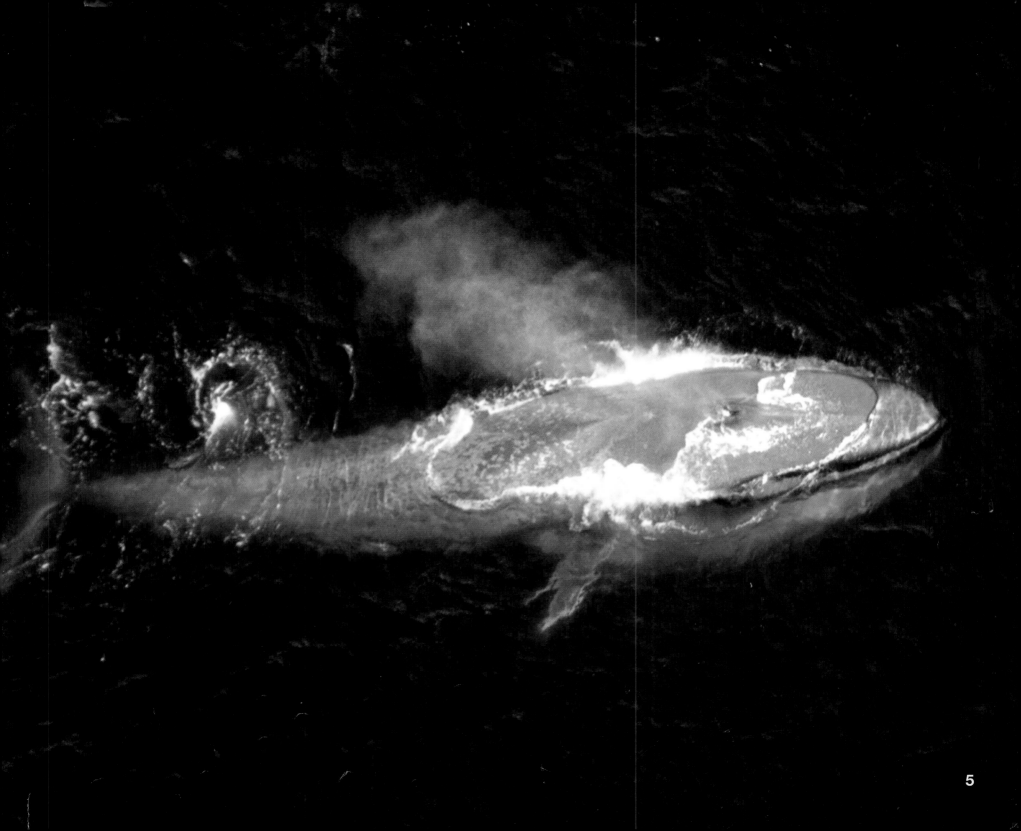

Swoosh! A polar bear's

giant paws dip into the water.

With one grab, the bear pulls

a 150-pound (70-kilogram) seal

onto the ice.

Crack! A jaguar snaps its jaws.
A jaguar's jaws and teeth
are strong enough to break
through a turtle's shell.

# Stronger

Swoosh! Eight strong arms

reach out to grab prey.

A North Pacific giant octopus

is strong enough to make

a shark its next meal.

Powerful!

An anaconda coils
its body around prey.
Its squeeze is as strong as
a 9,000-pound (4,100-kilogram)
school bus sitting on your chest.

A 9-pound (4-kilogram) crowned eagle may not be big. But its talons can snatch up monkeys and other prey four times its size.

# Strongest

An African elephant weighs

as much as 60 people.

This elephant is as

strong as it is big.

Its trunk can lift small trees!

SUPER HERO Strength!

Danger is near.

A male gorilla throws branches.

Predators beware!

This mammal is strong enough

to lift a small car.

Not all strong animals are big.

The rhinoceros beetle can carry

850 times its own weight.

Imagine carrying 850 friends

on your back!

# Glossary

extreme—very great

krill—tiny shrimplike animals

mammal—a warm-blooded animal with a backbone and hair or fur; female mammals feed milk to their young

predator—an animal that hunts other animals for food

prey—an animal that is hunted by another animal for food

talon—a sharp claw of a bird of prey such as an eagle, a hawk, or a falcon

# Read More

**Murray, Julie**. *Strongest Animals.* That's Wild! A Look at Animals. Edina, Minn.: ABDO Pub., 2010.

**Stout, Frankie**. *Nature's Strongest Animals.* Extreme Animals. New York: PowerKids Press, 2008.

# Internet Sites

FactHound offers a safe, fun way to find Internet sites related to this book. All of the sites on FactHound have been researched by our staff.

Here's all you do:

Visit *www.facthound.com*

Type in this code: 9781429653091

Super-cool stuff! Check out projects, games and lots more at
**www.capstonekids.com**

# Index

Word Count: 217
Grade: 1
Early-Intervention Level: 19